The Paradigm Shift

Introduction

Are you a paradigm shifter? In this social report, I remember my mother asking me to write a report on what would it take for us to restore the earth, become immortals and live sustainable lives as infinite beings? I thought to myself, is this a question that a woman as myself could answer? With the power of God, anointing of the Holy Spirit and the faith in the good news, Jesus Christ, I prayed, fasted and meditated day and night until I was able to build on the title she gave me, the name she gave this word of motivation, the Paradigm Shift.

The Underground Railroad

I started to ponder on the events of the world. I wondered what it would take for the future generations to be ready for Jesus. Is it possible to be covered by the Living God? I thought about the story of Enoch, who walked with God, and so he and his country walked with God, and they never were seen again. In this same, truth, the legends tell of Elijah and Moses, servants who walked with God, and the world saw them leave earth. As we ponder the opportunity to walk with God, we learn that the walk of God is not as easy as many think. The nations and populations come and go, and all have seen trials, tribulations, and often enough, some were buried, and some have been found missing and their bodies never found. The Underground Railroad made me think of this walk with God. The unique story of the construction of identity of the WALKER OF GOD.

Walker of God

I remember as a child in my imaginary world, I found GOD. God was my imaginary friend. Many thought this was not healthy. My communities did not want to hear me say that I was talking to GOD. As though, I was talking to GHOSTS, or having an imaginary friend, made it evident that I was a troubled child. In these years, I realize that the "WORD" came to life. I loved reading and listening to people speak words. These words became part of my imagination. I had such a strong imagination that I was able to visualize people's words as walking entities. This is what I called the Fantasy world. I remember when I created my first Fantasy World. I created from the fairies, fairy tales of the old that reminded me of the possibilities that we do not live alone, but the world was bigger than we expected. Why would we become paradigm shifters if we were destined to be extinct? We had hoped that immortality and infinity had to be a second chapter of the human soul. We looked into the waters of God, and thought we were part of a stronger element of life through God.

The Underground Railroad

Levi Coffin, (bio, 2015), was called the president of the Underground Railroad. His wealth afforded him to become the president of the Underground Railroad. He assisted over 3,000 slaves into freedom to the North into Canada. The Underground Railroad was a network of people who helped Harriet Tubman and others escape slavery by traveling a safe passage from house to house, or tree to tree to the freedom in North of the States and eventually some into

The PARADIGM SHIFT

Canada. It is not that Levi Coffin was the president of the Underground Railroad but a wealthy man who skillfully invested in the service to assist slaves to cross over as a safe house.

The actions that Harriet Tubman as the founder of the network system and routes, became a famous iconic transformative leader who motivated the Quakers to participate in the work. As the routes grew, safe houses were increased, and members were increased. Quakers as a church became involved as an organization, business, and investors of the Underground Railroad because they saw the slaves as God's children. Those who needed their aide.

Anderson Ruffin Abbott

The black Canadian physician had become member of the Underground Railroad. As a professional, he became investor in real estate, and as a land owner started

The PARADIGM SHIFT

to serve blacks into Canada by building communities that were safe for slaves who escaped. Anderson Ruffin Abbott became a physician and served the black communities, so they were able to receive equality through medical advantages, (Heritage Room, 2015).

The Routes

The New Millennium

In this statement, the paradigm shift was when people built a secret society that created a network that assisted slaves to find freedom through working together in unity to build a network of wealth, resources, talents, skills, and real estate to pursue the mission of safety, security and equality for all. This social change created a shift in the United States called the economic devastation. A population of skilled workers left the South, eventually left the North, and Canada had the wealth and riches of those workers. Let us look into how Canada treated these fugitive slaves.

Canada Fugitives

The Myths Told, (June & Writer, 2015),

> There was a hope that Canada would provide a safe haven for runaways after 1833, however. Slave owners attempted to frighten their property so the slaves would never seek this safe haven in Canada. The

slaves were told the river to freedom (the Detroit River) was three thousand miles wide. There were undoubtedly told of the terrors of Niagara. The myths continued and included vivid, yet wild, descriptions of barren land where only black eyed peas would grow. The most frightening story was that abolitionists were cannibals who would fatten, boil, and then dine on the runaways. The truth was

> not hidden for long since there was no ban on oral communication among slaves. The word of the "land of promise" quickly spread. (Hill, 25)

This reminded me of the stories of the Promise Land. How the Israelites had to cross the desert, war with a country to enter into a new chapter of freedom in the Promise Land. It was in this right passage, that the fugitives escaped the torture and terror of slavery in the South, who were mostly governed by a hate crime organization and secret society called the KKK (Ku Klux Klan). During these years of escape, the fugitives feared to go with these groups, eventually betraying and becoming secret agents to expose the routes, the members and the fugitives. It was a division with the fugitives and the slaves who lived in terror from their slave owners who tortured them to speak and expose the secret organization of those who were escaping.

The routes were a testament of today's controversial struggle with the sex trafficking and slave trafficking routes versus the routes of the Underground Railroad. People are representation of the Dark Matter and Light Matter of Atoms, Negative and Positive force, energy that creates these two worlds in earth. We are

The PARADIGM SHIFT

experiencing the labor pains of the mother that travail under her breath for freedom. I have collected some information Wikipedia, the community of principle investigators who have collected information, below are some tidbits of the collected data of these routes. Yes, many scholars, and institutions do not support the Wikipedia as a reliable source as a dictionary or encyclopedia, but I do not mind using these social change agency to create an expression of concern of our future prediction of terrorism, crisis and disaster brought to us through the atoms of negative and positive energy we must grow through the growing pains of a woman who travail of the manifestations of the freedom of her people and the bondage of her people.

Wikipedia Highlights

"Although the fugitives sometimes traveled on boat or train,[20] they usually traveled on foot or by wagon in groups of 1–3 slaves. Some groups were considerably larger. Abolitionist Charles Turner Torrey and his colleagues rented horses and wagons and often transported as many as 15 or 20 slaves at a time," (Wikipedia, 2015).

"Routes were often purposely indirect to confuse pursuers.

Most escapes were by individuals or small groups; occasionally, there were mass escapes, such as with the Pearl incident. The journey was often considered particularly difficult and dangerous for women or children. Children were sometimes hard to keep quiet or were unable to keep up with a group. In addition, female slaves were rarely allowed to leave the plantation, making it harder for them to escape in the same ways that men could.[22] Although escaping was harder for women, some women did find success in escaping. One of the most famous and successful abductors (people who secretly traveled into slave states to rescue those seeking freedom) was Harriet Tubman, an escaped slave woman." (Wikipedia, 2015).

"Due to the risk of discovery, information about routes and safe havens was passed along by word of mouth. Southern newspapers of the day were often filled with pages of notices soliciting information about escaped slaves and offering sizable rewards for their capture and return. Federal marshals and professional bounty hunters known as slave catchers pursued fugitives as far as the Canadian border." (Wikipedia, 2015).

What would it take to receive a new generation of policy and social growth? We have seen in business relations that companies are experiencing the freedom to create policy. The co-creators of social transformative development and morale maturity have pushed us all to question why are some moving toward the direction of freedom and others left behind in bondage and dysfunction. It

The PARADIGM SHIFT

is evident that our world is given the power and laws of attraction through association, but what more do we know about the energy force called the atoms of negative and positive movement?

> "These included Lower Canada (present-day Quebec) and Vancouver Island, where Governor James Douglas encouraged black immigration because of his opposition to slavery. He also hoped a

significant black community would form a bulwark against those who wished to unite the island with the United States. Upon arriving at their destinations, many fugitives were disappointed as life in Canada was difficult. While the British colonies had no slavery after 1834, discrimination was still common. Many of the new arrivals had to compete with mass European immigration for jobs, and overt racism was common. For example, in reaction to Black Loyalists being settled in eastern Canada by the Crown, the city of Saint John, New Brunswick amended its charter in 1785 specifically to exclude blacks from practicing a trade, selling goods, fishing in the harbor, or becoming freemen; these provisions stood until 1870.

The PARADIGM SHIFT

With the outbreak of the Civil War in the U. S., many black refugees left Canada to enlist in the Union Army. While some later returned to Canada, many remained in the United States. Thousands of others returned to the American South after the war ended. The desire to reconnect with friends and family was strong, and most were hopeful about the changes emancipation and

Reconstruction would bring."
(Wikipedia, 2015).

Paradigm Shift and the Shifters

What Did It Take?

The fact remains that the conditions of the fugitives were not collectively perfect, but it was livable that they were able to return to the United States to assist in the win over The Civil War, and the assistance of the Reconstruction of the United States. As you can see in the 21st

century, the reconstruction did not fully remove the parasite and viruses of overt and covert issues of racial conflict with communities that were estranged in hostility and violence against one another. The transference were in the policing of black citizens, poverty, poor quality medical attention, lack of resources in education, and verbal abuse, psychological oppression, and the distrust of their neighbor which were broken trust with family and friends in their own communities.

The division of race, gender and class did not get resolved in the States. The transference of the abolitionist movement and the civil rights movement transferred into the prison system, policing and legal, medical and education segregation, terrorism in the souls of the institutions, policies and practices of the employees, management and executives in all agencies. African Americans were faced with terror daily that their lives would be in jeopardy. People mocked them, persecuted them from the lack of resources, lack of education, lack of stability, creditability and the issues of skills became an issue when they worked long days, long nights, lack of parenting, and lack of retreat. The African Americans were locked in the heritage of losing integrity and inheritance due to policy and procedures of the institution. The wars against cultures became a normalcy

The PARADIGM SHIFT

that shifted a country in five countries. The country of the Native Americans, the country of the African Americans, the country of the Asian Americans, and the divided country of the European Americans and Aryan Americans that became the negative and positive energy of the American Dream. All other cultures became entangled by these racial confrontation of historical unsettling rests of betrayal, bondage, terror and broken promises and abuse.

The PARADIGM SHIFT

Why BE a Paradigm Shifter?

The Harriet Tubman, the conductor of the Underground Railroad. Many people spoke of her life as a lonely life, who lost everything and without compensation, appreciation, recognition and wealth, she made her last days in solitude, isolation and alienation from the world due to her fame and her search. People wonder why anyone would want to be a social agent or social agency for social change if it means

The PARADIGM SHIFT

the hardship of starvation, poverty, isolation and alienation, a life living in fear, overcoming fear, and the struggle to prove your sanity through the work that is invisible. The promise that people would love you, adore you and cherish you disappears as soon as the realization that the work is never done, and a dent has not been made, due to new populations, increased numbers that grew into this ignorance of support of wealth, waste and consumption.

The PARADIGM SHIFT

Watching the prison system, police brutality, terror sweep the streets, and lives of the same population who fought in the Civil War, the unsettling wrestling of identity and the liberation of any taxonomy of the wealth versus the poverty that is accumulated from historical holocausts of cultures trafficked into the country as slaves and not immigrants and professionals. It is with this report of social evolution that the morale maturity of a country

The PARADIGM SHIFT

promoted authoritarian conclusions that people who own properties, merchants who traded goods, and traders who worked the black markets to legally compromised, corrupt a system that are in favorable of free labor, under regulated prospects, conceive the destruction of a community and a future. It is with this report, the paradigm shift says, no. We have a future, and we can rise above the ashes, as phoenixes.

The PARADIGM SHIFT

The agencies began the journey to pursue the liberation for their own life and those who they consider as in need. People have found that non-profit organizations and non-profit corporations were recruited to serve communities who were estranged wives of the country. It was in that age 19th century that these social agencies wanted to build communities, but yet why were these communities still increasing, and the communities were still in terror, in psychological defective to change policies. What happened when they were given property, good income and a good life? What happened after they were served?

Terminology

"William Still,[26] often called "The Father of the Underground Railroad", helped hundreds of slaves to escape (as many as 60 a month), sometimes hiding them in his Philadelphia home.

He kept careful records, including short biographies of the people, that contained frequent railway metaphors. He maintained correspondence with many of them, often acting as a middleman in communications between escaped slaves and those left behind. He published these accounts in the book The Underground Railroad (1872), a valuable resource for historians to understand how the system worked and a recounting of individual ingenuity in escapes.

According to Still, messages were often encoded so that they could be understood only by those active in the railroad. For example, the following message, "I have sent via at two o'clock four large hams and two small hams", indicated that four adults and two children were sent by train from Harrisburg to Philadelphia. The additional word via indicated that the "passengers" were not sent on the usual train, but rather via Reading, Pennsylvania. In this case, the authorities were tricked into going to the regular train station in an attempt to intercept the runaways, while Still met them at the correct station and guided them to safety. They eventually escaped either to the

North or to Canada, where slavery had been abolished during the 1830s, (Wikipedia, 2015).

People are struggling now with language, terminology and how to use the conversation with the affluent and those in impoverish communities. The ethno-linguistics have been developed due to this issue of Proper English, Academic English, and the APA Styling. People are not able to finish college due to terminology, and the proper usage of terminology, vocabulary and structuring sentences within a voice. Students, workers, and citizens are given great wealth based on inheritance and terminology. People are segregated based on terminology. People are speaking codes daily. The language people speak can make them or break them in the society at large. We have seen in the African American communities that they are given excellent scores, and respect based on their ability to articulate the language given to them, which brings me to the point of the Underground Railroad. The terminology was successful due to the simplicity of the language. People were able to understand the roles of their leaders through the terminology used to guide the fugitives who had little to none understanding due to the segregation and isolation done to them by their owners.

Sexually violated, men and women were raped during the slavery age in the United States. People do not talk much about the countries neighboring the States, but racism were not recorded as it was recording in the United States. Many records were erased, as we are seeing in the current day. Organizations are not required to keep any documentation after five to seven years, yet we have seen our credit reports held for more than ten years. It is in this system we have found that the owners are given more freedom to erase their errors, while the underrepresented are accounted and accountable for their errors for life.

The paradigm shift begins in the heart of the human being. The day Enoch walked with GOD he changed his country by the guiding of the Holy Spirit, and the Son of God. WE believe that it is evident that the Underground Railroad was not the first social agency or social change, but the first had to be in the life of Enoch, Elijah and Moses. These three founding fathers were what we called the Underground Railroad to Heaven. It was with this sense that we have two Underground Railroads, one on earth and one in heaven.

Much like the Underground Railroad, Harriet Tubman, as conductor, served fugitives to get to the stations, and to cross over without being captured by owners, and the organizations that worked against the slaves. This was a very dangerous movement due to the violence and

The PARADIGM SHIFT

terrorism done against the slaves and those who helped the slaves. Illegally they were tried, killed, and sometimes, not making to the court system, and not given the appropriate due process for restorative justice, the affluent, the owners, and those who had protection under the law, still remained in the luxury to kill, steal and destroy lives that were innocent and forgettable by their world.

Wikipedia High lights:

The PARADIGM SHIFT

Members of the Underground Railroad often used specific terms, based on the metaphor of the railway. For example:

People who helped slaves find the railroad were "agents" (or "shepherds")

Guides were known as "conductors"

Hiding places were "stations"

The PARADIGM SHIFT

"Station masters" hid slaves in their homes

Escaped slaves were referred to as "passengers" or "cargo"

Slaves would obtain a "ticket"

Similar to common gospel lore, the "wheels would keep on turning"

Financial benefactors of the Railroad were known as "stockholders"

Conclusion

The PARADIGM SHIFT

In this case, people are forged into the belief system of fear, to make a change, to go against their owners. In the 21st century we are not legally owned, but we are fearful of losing security, safety and happiness, and that has become our own jail cells, concentration camps, and terrorism. We have become mentally trapped in the decisions of TO obtain a TICKET or to BECOME CARGO.

In this report, I challenge you to becoming ENOCH, ELIJAH and

The PARADIGM SHIFT

MOSES, as Station Masters, Agents, Stations or Conductors. People are not looking any longer for friendships, but people are looking for safe passage. Financial benefactors of the Railroad, stockholders who are willing to "WHEELS WOULD KEEP ON TURNING.

In order for us to become a new generation of a forge against negative atoms, transformative leadership must ask themselves what is a paradigm

The PARADIGM SHIFT

shift or a paradigm shifter? And am I one of them.

Coach Kay

Keisha Lanell Merchant

Tried by the Fire, Coaching Communities, Businesses, Institutions, Individuals and Agencies, Agents how to practice, perform and perfect the green techniques to manifest and advance in biotechnology, double swing communications and the North Star stakeholders.

If you want me to train, coach and educate your corporate culture, communities, build your community, agency, and want to pay for my services, travel, and my team to build you and your population; please contact my agency:

merchatchatterbox@gmail.com

503-479-5493 or find me on Twitter, Linkedin, Facebook or Google.

The PARADIGM SHIFT

One Love, Much Love

EII ☺

www.ingramcontent.com/pod-product-compliance
Lightning Source LLC
Chambersburg PA
CBHW051821170526
45167CB00005B/2103